Made in United States
North Haven, CT
15 November 2021

11174245R00068